ARE YOU ACTUALLY GOING TO WRITE A BOOK OR JUST TALK ABOUT IT?

An aggressive guide to writing, creativity, and actually getting things done.

BRANDON SCOTT

Everyone who's ever asked me how I wrote so many books,

Who's held a story in their hearts,

Every aspiring novelist,

This one's for you.

WORDS FOR THE WEARY ARTIST

Perhaps it's the first time someone's told you these words—but I hope not. And even if they have, you deserve to hear them again.

You're okay.

You're important.

It may not seem like it some days, but you're the future.

You're what gives me hope for this species. You're proof this planet deserves to exist.

You are not just a product of culture.

You are culture.

Writers, my family. Bound by something more important than blood. You give this world its stories. You make people's lives lose its mundanity and make dreams coherent.

Musicians, my friends. You give this world hope and joy. You take the heaviness of existence and turn it into a beautiful song. You give emotions sound.

Actors, my heroes. You give art a face. You become conduits for characters, and stories, and beliefs. You make us laugh, and cry. You make us feel again.

Singers, my inspiration. You prove humans do indeed have a soul. You prove it every time you sweep away the world with just your voice.

Everyone else. If I had the time, I would describe how much each of you matter. You painters, and sculptors, and poets, and anyone I've forgotten. And any new types yet to grace this world.

I'm going to repeat that again.

You matter.

You matter.

YOU matter.

I know sometimes it does not seem like it. I know at the beginning it can feel like the world is against you. That even your family and friends are against you. And it can be hard. It can be so hard sometimes. The urge to quit is present in even the most dedicated artists.

But please don't.

It's only so hard because it's important. It's only so hard because it tests us. We are creating something from nothing. That is an act of the divine. That is a gift from something greater than our bodies. Greater than anything else.

So, create. Create because you were born to do it. Create because it burns inside you with a fire.

Create so you might yet find immortality.

Contents

Prelude 1:

WHAT IS THIS BOOK, AND WHY SHOULD I CARE?

Hello, hi, and howdy. The name is Brandon Scott (though you already knew that) and the point of this book is in the goddamn title. But I'm still going to explain what you just bought, what you have in your hands, and what the intent of this is.

I feel like it will go better for all of us if you go into this without any wrong ideas.

So, first off, this is not a book to make you famous. This is not a book to allow you to quit your day job and become a bestselling author. This book will not change your life or anything. I can't even promise that someone is going to buy anything you write.

No, the point of this book is to put, in one place, years of knowledge learned about the art of writing books and doing it well. The point of this book is to make it so that people who have been meaning to write a book and just never managed can finally, *finally* get the first draft of their book written.

When you are a professional writer (and yes, I am that) the most common thing you hear when you tell people your job is that they want to write a book. Commonly, they'll even have managed a chapter or two or are a few thousand words into their first attempt.

The thing is, these kinds of books will never be finished. They won't even get to a first draft. The vast majority of people who set out to write a book will never achieve it.

And this is not a value judgment, and I don't want you to think of it as a slight against your character. The fact is that most people are not writers, but everyone thinks they can write a book. The fact is that even the people who could be writers, who have the imagination and the work ethic and the temperament, are still stifled. They often do not have the right information about how to *finish* a book.

Let me make this one point very clear: starting a book, thinking of an idea for a book, is immensely easy. I can do it in an hour, on a bad day.

Finishing a single draft is a wall, a herculean task, and one that is not fun, is not glamorous, and is not easy. It can take years, it can ruin relationships, it can mess up people's mental and physical well-being. To do what it sometimes takes to get a book to a first draft is not easy in the normal world.

That's why people often give up on it. Not because they are weak, but because writing a book is time consuming, and finding time is hard if you are not financially well off or supported by someone.

But, if you spent your few dollars for this book, you might already know that. And you want help so that you can actually get a book done anyway.

So, let's go over how you are going to really, actually *write* this book of yours.

Prelude 2:

HOW TO ACTUALLY USE THIS BOOK FOR SOMETHING.

The thing about these kinds of books is that you likely will give up before you finish it. You won't listen to me or disagree with my words, or simply life will get in the way and you'll forget about this book.

And this is where the tough love portion comes in on you, dear reader. Because I expect a good chunk of the people who buy this book to still fail. I expect you to not follow through and not do all that you need to do to *actually write a damn book* and end up at square one, looking for a different self-help book to get you through this.

And you know what? If that other book does work for you, then I'm glad. My way is not the only way (far from it), and I don't much care if I'm personally the nail in the coffin that finally tips you over to be an author. My goal is two-fold: to get people closer to success, and to get the few people who really benefit from my teachings to complete the lifelong goal that is writing a book.

But, if you're going to read this book, then you are going to follow it my way, and my way is not an easy walk in the park—but it is a very effective way. I'm putting out this book and offering it for sale with the intent for you to do as this book says.

But, before that, full disclosure: this book is not wholly new material from me. For you see, among my many writing-related tasks and projects, I'm a blogger. And a blogger who has written a metric fuck-ton of content already on the subject of being a writer and learning to write.

So, I'm reusing stuff. This book is a structured compendium of lessons, musings, and hard-won truths about writing put in one place, and arranged in such a way as to teach you how to write a book.

It is meant to be read in the order I present it. Don't jump ahead, or skip around, even if you feel like you are ahead of a certain level or beyond what I am talking about—you bought my book, so let me teach you my way.

I'm going to give you short, easy-to-read articles that cover general concepts.

I want you to read them in full.

I'm going to give you assignments.

I want you to do them *before you read anything more in the book unless I tell you otherwise!*

I am going to throw around some writerly terms, and use slang, and maybe pepper in some words that you have never seen before.

I am expecting *you* to use the magic that is the internet to research anything you've never heard of and make sure you understand what I am talking about.

Cool?

Okay, let's get started on this.

HOW TO START BEING A WRITER: A GUIDE FOR ABSOLUTE BEGINNERS

So, I hear you want to be a word-slinger? That you want to dance with a little lady named fiction? Well, for all of you who still call themselves "aspiring writers," here are a few steps for the absolute beginning of your journey.

Because while there may be plenty of places offering tips on publishing, or writing your first novel, I thought I would share with you some *advice* on how to begin this crazy writer life.

1. Stop Calling Yourself An "Aspiring Writer."

If you write, you're a writer. Endpoint, done. If you're really serious about this whole writing thing, then call yourself a writer. Own that title.

2. Set Aside Time

And now comes the first hard part. At any age, and even if writing is your occupation, you will still need to find time to work on writing. And I'm sorry to say that for beginners it's going to be the time you usually play video games or watch television. This is a sacrifice you're going to have to make.

3. Find A Quiet Space

Some writers like writing to music. I too find it a good way to get myself pumped up beforehand (though I sometimes will turn it off while I'm actually writing,) and that's okay. But I can guarantee that you are not going to appreciate random loud noises. So, find a nice secluded place to get the words going.

4. Start A Blog

Okay, now you get to do the actual work part of all of this.

"But why a blog?" I hear you ask.

It's quite simple, blogging on a schedule will teach you two things real quick:

- How to not rely on inspiration,
- And how to let go.

Articles will have to come out every week/month/day, regardless of how you feel. You can edit them beforehand as hard as you want, but they will never be perfect.

Never, ever.

But you'll still put them out there.

You'll still have to let other people see it.

This might be the most important step. It's what separates the serious from amateurs.

5. Set A Word Target

This does not include blog articles. I repeat, do not count the words in your articles.

Got it?

Okay.

Every day, or at least every weekday, you have to write a certain amount of words. They can be fiction; they can be whatever you want. Do not edit them while you are writing them. Just keep going. If your word processor marks something as misspelled, you can fix that. But nothing else.

You'll edit it later.

Now, how many words should you do? Here's my advice: start with 300. If you find yourself repeatedly going over that because you're so into whatever you're working on, raise the target by 300.

Rinse, repeat, keep to it. It's like physical training, there will be days where you'll have to push yourself.

But damn is it satisfying.

6. **Finally, Have Fun**

Despite how serious the whole article's been, above all: have fun. Art is supposed to be fun. Creation is fucking magic. Treat your art form with respect but enjoy it as well.

Sure, there'll be hard days. Hard weeks. Hard months even. I'm not saying it's going to be easy. But as long as the feeling of being a writer, a creator of worlds, fills you with happiness, then keep at it.

Because this world needs artists. Artists like you.

WHY YOU SHOULD WRITE ALL THE DAMN TIME

Alright beginners, let me tell you the magic secret to becoming a better writer.

"WRITE A LOT AND READ A LOT."

No, don't you dare. I see you raising your hand in the back. I see you scoffing at me and rolling your eyes. You, slinking behind the buffet bar, don't even try to run. The metaphorical door is locked and guarded, and I hid the key underneath my hat.

So, sit down. All of you. Let me disillusion you of some notions.

###

"I DON'T WANT TO WRITE UNTIL I'M INSPIRED."

I shudder when I hear you say that. It's not "write when you're inspired," it's "write UNTIL inspiration hits, and then keep going." People let their muse control them when actually you control your muse. She's sitting inside your head, twiddling her thumbs, and waiting for you to give her something to work with. Those little random bursts of creativity are her getting fed up and clawing at your brainpan.

"I DON'T WANT / LIKE / HAVE TIME TO READ."

Seriously? The birth of a writer starts with a person who loves to read. So, if you're against it, I think you need to come up with a different goal. It's not even hard to do. Books are the best choice, but if none are available then read articles and blogs. The important thing is that you consume words like it keeps you alive. Because it sort of does.

"I'VE GOT WRITER'S BLOCK."

Okay fine. I get it. You're stuck on something in your current project. It happens. So, write something else! Anything else! Short stories, essays, poems, reviews, love letters, songs, or even your will. Just write something! Anything!

"BUT I'M NOT ANY GOOD AT WRITING."

Neither was I. Art takes practice. It takes a *lot* of practice. That's why you have to write all the goddamn time. Writing constantly will teach you technique, it will teach you what works and what doesn't. It will let you find your voice. It will teach you how to continue to be inspired. It will show you what kind of person you are.

It will make you confident in what you are doing. It will make you into a goddamn artist.

Ignore the guy crying in the corner. I think I broke his mind. For the rest of you, do you understand now? Do you feel the twitch in your fingertips you've ignored for so long?

Good! Then go write some words.

BAD WRITER HABITS

I meet a lot of people, a depressing amount of people, who could be writers. They have an innate understanding of a compelling construction and possess a creative drive and an imagination beyond normal.

But, as other writers immortalized, "writers are people who write," and these people I meet often don't write beyond random ineffective bouts of literary flailing. And it hurts me: this loss of potential. I see the spark unused. I had that same spark, and someone else recognized it and got me going—and I wish I could do that for these people. Be a mentor or a colleague. Get the energy flowing.

But as they move in the right direction—if they even make it past the fear of beginning—they stumble onto bad habits. Brutally bad habits. And no matter how much advice I give, how much time devoted to helping them, if they do not unlearn these habits, they won't earn the title of a serious writer.

They just won't.

And it's a real problem. Because, though I am not connected to other artistic groups like I am with writing (I don't know a great number of painters, or illustrators, and only a few dancers and actors), I must imagine that barriers exists for those who pursue those pursuits and stops hundreds of thousands of creatives in their tracks.

What's probably the problem is the habits seem so intuitive. The natural operational parameters of the average person are a crippling thing to the production of artistic endeavors.

And don't, I repeat: DON'T, do these things, but I will list them for the sake of education and for your enjoyment.

Don't wait for an idea.

You are not a slave of inspiration. You are its master. Whip your inspiration into shape by plowing through its roadblocks, and it will learn to give gifts whenever you demand it to do so.

Don't abandon stories halfway.

I don't care how shitty it is. Do not leave a project half-written. You can only fix what is already there. Get a first draft done, at least. Stopping halfway through makes it easier to quit on other projects. And then you will never finish anything creative.

Don't talk about the story you want to write.

Write the story you want to write. Don't say it. A story is a communication, an expression of ideas and concepts and emotions. If you say your story, aloud, to anyone besides yourself, then you already communicated. And you will have a heck of a harder time writing the story down.

Don't show people the first draft of anything.

I get it, you're proud of your work. But, honestly, if you show someone your first attempts, you will more than likely get criticism. And, for the beginner, criticism is a killer of drive. Once you have some semblance of self-confidence in your creative ability, you will not be at risk of breaking down from a single nasty comment. So, hold off until that time comes.

Don't buy big tools right off the bat.

Excitement is good. Excitement is awesome. Inspiration is an (unnecessary) enjoyable thing. But and I am not sure why this is the case, buying all the big toys right off the bat results in never using the toys. Like with exercise equipment, having a treadmill will not make you walk more. Having been a dedicated walker makes the tool useful: the tool does not make you into a dedicated walker. The same seems to hold true of many things—writing included.

Don't start off with a book.

Seriously. Write shorts first. One hundred words, five pages, ten pages—something, anything easier. A book is an odd thing: once you do it once, you can do it again and again. But, it's still a wall, and it's a wall that trying to run right into, as your first step, results in often nothing but a busted nose and dashed dreams.

####

These are all bad habits people have. Some people succeed despite such things, but, for the majority, if you want to be a creative: unlearn—as fast as you can— doing these actions. Use what simple tools you have, the simpler the better in fact, and just make some stuff. Then repeat for more time than you'd think reasonable, and you'll see your mental muscles grow strong enough to hold yourself up and push away the walls that hold you inside their granite arms.

There's no easy way. It's work. It's practice. It's not at all for everyone.

But more people should create. And bad habits are something standing in the way of that.

GOOD WRITER HABITS

Okay, so, if you keep up with my newest posts, then you would know I recently covered a bunch of bad habits a lot of wannabe writers seem to have that makes them crash and burn before they really begin. And, in the interest of not only being negative, I thought I would offer some helpful habits that if used will—possibly—increase your comfort toward writing, and your output as a writer. Your mileage may vary of course, and some of these may seem outrageously obvious, but you'd be surprised how many times I've told these things to "almost writers," and they did little to follow them.

Writing is about discipline, after all, and these actions take that same discipline to accomplish. But though that might sound scary, they are not too hard to do, really. And, from them comes useful fruit.

So, with all that preamble gone and done, here we go.

Read a bit every day.

Just, like, read a *little*. I watch television; I go see movies. Distractions aplenty reach me like everyone else. But, to write, you must know what other's writing is like. Not doing that is writing blind—like baking a cake when you've never eaten cake. I'm not saying 50 pages a day, or a book a week. You don't need to do something huge. I mean read like 10-20 pages every night before bed. That's all. You'll finish a novel a month at that clip, and if you are a traveling person who has no time for a bulky paperback or a heavy hardcover, well, the world has e-books and audiobooks now, so there's no real excuse.

Exercise a bit a day.

A half-hour is enough. Walk around your block a few times. Go for a calm stroll. Motion gets the brain going and being outside like that is a great time for brainstorming if nothing else.

Write every day.

You know this one. I am including it so you remember it is something you should do. Again, like reading, only a little is needed if that's all you have time for in your busy life. If you do not stop to self-edit (which is a no-no), 250 words can take under five minutes, even if you do not know how to type.

Finish a mini project every week.

Sometimes this is not feasible. But, finishing—and by "finishing," I mean writing, revising, editing, and proofreading to completion—something, even if it is only like 300 words, is a great way to build up muscles that will come in handy later when working with a full book. Plus, learning to manage deadlines is a good skill to have in general, even if you only write as a hobby.

Daydream.

This is for motivation's sake. In the word mines, it can all seem endless. The task too much to bear. So—though don't get a swelled head—doing a *little* daydreaming about people liking your book, and reading your stories, can help keep you motivated. Do not write for fame or glory—those are not common in the literary world—but *do* imagine it being a possible future. Because it *is* possible.

Good habits can make good routines and *can* make good writers. So, if you want to go at this writing thing harder than you've done before, consider adopting into your life a few—not that difficult—habits. I'd recommend all of them, as they build on each other, but, if that's too strenuous: take at least the first three for a spin.

After all, what can it hurt?

Assignment 1:

No points for figuring out what the assignment is going to be here. The articles you just read probably already gave you an idea of it, but here are the most important parts. You can continue reading this book once you've set yourself up to keep in these routines, but only once you're committed to doing them. Aim to consistently do these things for at least one week without failure, then try for two weeks, and so on until it becomes a habit and part of your daily life.

Blogging

1. Start a blog. Yes, really. It can be private at first but set a schedule for yourself (once a week is pretty good) and write a small article about anything on your mind. They can be anywhere from very short to mammoth length. It doesn't matter. Remember that anything you put on the internet is no longer private, so always be careful of revealing personal data or even people's first names.

2. If you haven't already, start making your blog articles available somewhere to read. There are plenty of places you can do that for free or near free.

3. Once you have written at least two (2) articles, checked them for grammar errors, and posted

them, *actively promote it* so that people you know (and ideally people you don't) read it.

4. Turn on comments for those posts. Do not read them but be aware when they happen.

Fiction/Non-Fiction Writing

1. Figure out, ideally, a few different smaller projects you can do. Short stories, specific memories you'd like to put to paper, anything like that. Don't plan a book yet. Just figure out stuff you can finish within a few days of writing.

2. Set a daily writing target. 300 words is the bare minimum. Don't go lower than that. Go as high as your schedule can allow.

3. Get your word count done every single day, without fail. You do not have to like the words you write, so long as you hit that word count. If you do fail, then don't beat yourself up, just get back into the routine immediately.

4. Do not post these stories or writings online. Do not show them to anyone but your most trusted friends and family. Most people's first attempts suck, and your future self will be *haunted* by you sharing some of this stuff if you do. After a few months, if you want to revisit them to see if they're any good, then go ahead. But wait at least three months.

Reading

1. Go and buy/find copies of every book you loved as a child. It doesn't matter what reading level it is. Children's books are wonderful, and stories meant for teens often hold more truth and wisdom than things for adults. Rereading classics you loved isn't just for nostalgia, it's rediscovering the core stories that likely got you to want to be a writer. Embrace these stories and remember why stories are so wonderful.

2. Read at least twenty (20) pages a day. If you find that you don't have time to do this, then *find a simpler book for younger readers.* I'm not kidding. You *can* find the time to read twenty pages of a picture book meant for toddlers, for sure. Stuff for middle schoolers have not a lot on each page, so you can do it in five minutes. It is not beneath you to read simple books. No book is beneath you for the purposes of learning.

3. If you end up finishing a book mid your twenty-page read for the day, then pick up another book and finish the page count.

4. Read different kinds of books in different genres. Read romance if you like horror and historical adventure if you like romance. You can read more in your preferred genres, sure, but there is not a book in existence you can't learn something from, even if it's just how not to write a book or a scene.

That's a lot, huh? Sorry, but this first step is going to be the thing that tests if you mean it when you say you want to be a writer. This stuff is the absolute beginning of the track, the basic training you'll need to be able to write a book and get to the end.

If you can't do this, then you are not going to have any success with the latter parts.

If you are incapable of doing this, *then you are going to fail.*

These specific tasks are not necessarily essential, but if you can't get them done, then what hope is there to writing an entire book?

The following section is going to be a lot of advice about general fiction writing. The intent is to make the above steps easier to handle, so read the next section now, but they are not going to teach you how to keep in personal discipline and how to be motivated to keep writing.

That's got to come from you and keep coming from you.

YOU NEED ONLY LOOK

If you're a writer in need of some story ideas, or a new creative that is interested in coming up with an idea for your first creation, or even someone experiencing some kind of block—though I'm not one to believe in writer's block—then the advice I give is simple, the way forward is not complicated.

Look.

Most people don't see, they peer blindly at things; they pass along past, they automatically navigate through the usual stimuli—but there is a benefit in taking a second to look closer, to see the shaving marks on the tollbooth keeper's face, to wonder what caused the slight crease in the frosting on a coffee shop cupcake.

Imagination needs fuel, something to make magical, or scientific, or horrific. So, take a moment, and wonder about what something is and why it is that way. See the impossible and then make it real on paper. It's not hard—it's something we all know how to do; we have since we were little kids.

Some people just lost the ability to perceive and mold dreams so they overlap with reality. Most people have a spark of artistry in them—and can regain it by simply seeing what's around them, and how it *could* be. A painter can capture a moment and make it more. So can a photographer.

We writers can formulate a tale from a simple scene.

I'm all for computer screens—I love technology—but taking a walk outside every day, or as often as weather permits, makes sure that I get a place where I can think. A wide-open sky and a world alive do wonders for you. It can do amazing things for problem-solving and stress and creative slumps.

Seriously, give it a try.

Our planet is absolutely bursting with stories and characters. Take the best of it, what sings to your soul, strain it through your perspective, and tell the world what you saw, but made as new and as wild as you please.

ON INSPIRATION
AND WHAT TO DO WITH IT

An interesting thing happened to me on Sunday night, and in my attempts to be more personal and open with you guys, I thought I'd share it with you.

I became inspired. I met inspiration. The taskmaster and—though often not permanent—companion of the working artist. And like a bomb blast in my head, a story came to me.

It was funny. I was at a play, and right in the middle of it, a single sentence slammed into my head so fucking hard that I nearly said it aloud. It echoed and made my eyes wide with excitement.

And once I got home—after some discussions with fellow artists—I stayed up till 4:30 A.M. making sure it came out of my head and onto paper.

And I'm sorry to say it's not something I can share with you guys, at least not right now. It's a big project. And who knows where I'll go with it. But this whole thing got me thinking about a couple of things. But mostly about inspiration.

Because, well, it's not always a thing we talk about is it? It's not something teachable. Or quantifiable. Writing is a disciplined art and learning to work without a muse is essential. But sometimes we do get a large burst of creativity. Sometimes we do get the almost play-disrupting brainchild.

And when that happens, what should we do with it?

Well, it may not be the same for you, but what I've learned, and what I do: is instead of launching into just writing the thing, I pour all of that spark into an outline. I mark down the whole plot. I make a future roadmap and a concise construction.

And then, once I know where I'm going with it, I get the discipline part in and get the shit *done*. A day at a time.

Because, believe it or not, inspiration is just another tool to wield. A not predictable tool, certainly. But also, certainly, not your boss.

WRITING CAN BE BORING
(AND THAT'S OKAY)

There's a thing known by those of us who have written a novel. And, it's a controversial thing. Not something widely shouted or thrown into the cosmos for all to hear. But it is true: no matter how hard to believe. And, you may get mad at me for saying this, but, here's the gist: writing, making art, creating stuff, is often a little boring.

It's taxing. It's hard. Art takes a long time—and with no guarantee that the result will be any good.

This, this fact, is why I preach discipline so much. Why I try to instruct new writers to just get that word count *done*. Because, besides things like self-editing and self-doubt being easy ways to kill the creative drive, if you go into a project assuming every second will be a rollicking good time, then you are in for a terrible surprise, mate.

Writing a book takes weeks, months, *years*. You are putting word after word after word, and no matter how much effort you put into plotting and outlining, you will end up with odd divergences and strange tangents. Where you're going isn't always obvious. You are walking a *lonely* road, and though you dream and hope for the end of the tunnel, you still must walk in the dark for a long time.

And, sure, that may sound exhilarating to some. Like barreling toward an unknown horizon. But, if you've taken a long road trip on the interstate as I have, you understand that no matter how exciting the destination may be, you will spend a huge amount of time passing dull fields and monotonous forests. Tons of sights which, after a while, make you sure your mind is melting out of your ears.

Now, the detractors to this statement, the ones who take offense to such a claim, probably don't understand that if you only write when excited about the writing, when you only write when the creative fire burns in your fingertips, you will *never* finish a book. Unless you bang out the entire creation during one bout of artistic explosion: you are dealing with long term *work*.

Writing (and all art) *is* work. That is another shattering statement, which I am sure some will not be happy about, but it is the truth. If making art is overwhelmingly easy all the time you are on a sure-to-end hot streak.

This may sound harsh, but that's only so I can clarify that what an artist does *is* work. It's some of the most respectable work on this planet, a supremely noble pursuit....

But it is not easy.

And it is not always fun.

The criminal sin of writing is to bore the reader, but just because you must do all you can to not bore your audience, you, as the artist being bored, is par for the course. So, expect boredom, and remember you are not experiencing a "block" or something of that ilk when it occurs. You are in the process of dragging something into reality from your *fucking mind*, and sometimes it gets a little stuck in the pipeline.

So, when the sense of tedium strikes, grit your teeth, and drag the sucker out, and don't believe for a second it means there's something wrong with you. You'll find art at the end of that tunnel, you'll find a voice, and—in the thematic blood and plot marrow of the work— you'll find what you care about most in the whole world.

But it won't always be exciting getting there.

THE KNOWLEDGE
YOU'VE GOT TO FORGET

As a nerd, and a "scholar of life" (if I may finally, *finally* reach peak pretentiousness), I've learned an important lesson for people—and artists especially.

And, before I go forward, a warning: It's hard to apply.

Really fucking hard.

But, it's also an admired quality.

It's something, that when someone has it, you notice from a mile away.

And it's kind of simple: to dance like no one is looking.

Metaphorically and literally.

The absolute best people are the ones who can do wild things. Put themselves out there in the oddest and weirdest ways. Express joy physically, exuberantly.

They are making the world better.

I'm friends with a lot of actors and singers and dancers, and the ability to do something like that, to be free with motion and expression, in real-time, it's amazing. I can only do it from behind a screen, with words I can edit.

The most powerful words are those told out loud and honestly, so honest they hurt the speaker to say them.

Conversations that touch on things that are so deep they are part of the soul are the only real conversations worth having.

And we all know when we are in those moments.

But, how to be that way?

Well…

The trick is to forget that the world is a judging place. A place that will smite you for doing what it does not deem acceptable. Forget, for a moment, that the world has consequences, that words can echo, that feelings do not really fade if they are important or personal, and simply do the thing anyway.

I have posted on this blog many things that, to this day, I wonder if they will bite me at some later date. That they were too open, too vulnerable, too crude, or too biased politically. It's frightening when you know nothing dies on the internet. You see so many stories about old words or ideas or statements screwing someone over years down the road. I write *dark* stuff sometimes—I tend to go a little far in my stories—and I am aware that, maybe, someday, I might get judged and attacked.

But I do this anyway.

I may not be brave enough to really dance with my whole body in public, when the music plays, when other's move their bodies, but I am brave enough to put my thoughts down on paper.

And years down the road, I may not agree with all I say now. But I still say it now.

To stay sane, to survive, I forget what I posted. Push it right out of my mind. Literally forget potential dangers and failure willfully.

Lying to yourself is not always a bad thing.

Sometimes we all need to forget that the world is cruel.

So that we might do something about it.

FUCK THAT LITTLE VOICE

Imposter syndrome, fear of criticism, and creative blocks. Some more legitimate than others, but all real. I would know, I've had them. *But*, despite being a nervous, introverted, lessening-so-but-still-shy person, I've done a good enough job of being out there with my artistic work.

Those issues I listed come down to a little voice telling us we are failures, that we are about to get shanked by the world at large for our lack of talent. And, while I don't know how to make myself able to tell a speech to a crowd, I have advice for how to slay this beast of a voice.

The trick is to adopt a careful, artistic, weighted idea of fuck it all. Does your first draft have problems? Fuck it all. Write each new chapter, each new version of an article, each variant of a speech, in a new document, and don't you dare look back. Copy it when you need to edit and rip the new version apart—but don't even consider it, recall it, ruminate on it, until you are ready to tear that creation a new hole.

Once you post something: never read it again. Unless you are actively trying to see your own flaws. But, if that is your intent, I can tell you this: that's an unnecessary step.

You'll find your own flaws well enough without gazing back. You'll recall those errors subconsciously anyway and other people will point it out to you.

Give a creation all your care, heart, and attention when you are doing it. Then, once it is out—unless you need to interact with the work for, say, marketing purposes—think of it not. Your art is yours—it is your soul—but you must leave your creations for *others* to enjoy, to pick apart.

The voice needs ammo. Bury that ammo in new things. Out-do doubt. It will never go away—I hear it all the time. Uncertainty is eternal. But skill and practice give you a counter-argument stronger and stronger enough to shove that fucker back down where it belongs.

Every post, book, article, poem sent out into the world is proof against that tiny voice.

That *it* is *not* your owner.

WRITING FLASH FICTION AND OTHER SUNDRY ADVICE

Lesson #1: Have A Theme

This might seem a bit basic, but that's because it's critical to your story. You only have a limited amount of space, so you need to focus on that one thing you want to get across. That does not mean your story needs to beat the person over the head with a theme, just make sure there *is* one. Whether your theme is death, love, paranoia, or my personal favorite: madness, you need to keep to just that theme, making sure to cut anything that doesn't help support or expand upon it. It's the only way you are going to fit your story into the 1,000-word limit.

Never tell people your theme. It's way more fun that way.

Lesson #2: Keep It to One or Two Protagonists

Due to the word limit, you need to keep to only a few characters. You really should have only one protagonist, but if you are crafty, you might be able to manage to balance two different character perspectives. Anything beyond that is a bit chaotic.

I will admit to personally breaking this rule. Very specific kinds of flash fiction can manage to have a lot of characters. Those sorts of stories usually revolve around a single event being viewed by different perspectives. Otherwise, it's best kept simple.

Lesson #3: Imply What You Can't Show

Believe it or not, you *can* world-build in flash fiction, you just have to be *really* sneaky about it. Attempting to use exposition is not feasible within 1,000 words, so you have to imply. Tell the reader about the world and the location strictly through contextual cues.

There are a lot of ways to do this, but dialogue is by far the most effective. Having characters offhandedly refer to events or objects during a conversation is a great way to clue people in on what exists in the story (just make sure not to be too heavy-handed about it). In science fiction or fantasy stories, this is incredibly useful because you can force the reader to automatically paint a world *around* the narrative.

Another is character reactions. If a character reacts to something, we would normally find outlandish in a calm way, then we can immediately assume that either it is totally mundane in their world, or the character is special.

Flash fiction *can* have as rich a narrative as anything else, it just takes some literary trickery.

Lesson #4: Fiction Rules Still Apply

All the normal rules still apply. All of them. Your story must have a beginning, a middle, and an end. It must have a protagonist. It needs to have a climax. Set up Chekhov's Guns and make sure to fire them.

Flash fiction is still fiction, it's just super condensed fiction.

Lesson #5: Start as Close to The Climax as Possible

By the climax, I mean whatever big action occurs in your story. An argument, a fight, a death, a kiss, whatever. Due to how much space you have, you need to start as close to the climax as you can. Because, generally speaking, that is the part that most people are reading for. In a book, you have a lot of time to set up various motivations and such beforehand.

You don't have that here.

All of that stuff *has* to come across before and *during* the climax, through implication.

Lesson #6: Don't Listen to Rules

The obligatory statement that everyone knows. You don't need to follow what I say.

You're an artist! Write flash fictions however the hell you want.

I simply offer you advice.

And my final piece of it is to ignore my advice.

If you can make a story that doesn't follow any of these rules and still is excellent and entertaining, then more power to you.

Because, honestly, fuck the rules.

Assignment 2:

It is time to write longer things. If you've been doing what I've told you to, then you're likely finding that occasionally you naturally write longer stories or longer posts. Now, we are going to train you to handle *consistently* longer stories.

You're still building up to a book, but this is a real step. Maintaining one world, one story, one set of characters is a bigger challenge and one that takes practice to handle.

So, here's your next task.

1. Dream up a story that will take you 5000 words to write.
2. Break that idea down into distinct scenes, or events, or plot actions, that will get you to the end of the story. Put them in a list format in a place you can look at as you write.
3. Figure out character names, occupations, and how they all are personally connected (or not personally connected) to each other and write that down in the same place. Make each character's name start with a different letter of the alphabet. Trust me, this will make things easier.

4. Don't try to tie this into other stories you've written or use characters from the book I know you're itching to write.

5. Don't plan to kill every character. You'd be amazed how often this is the impulse, but it's too easy and kind of lazy and makes it so you don't have to think of a proper ending.

6. Go ahead and read all the articles beyond this one *up to* the next assignment, they are a looser collection of writing advice and advice about being a creative person in the modern world.

7. Come back and look over your outline and adjust it to what you've learned, if needed. Yes, I may be making you redo your outline. Seeing any differences is important to understanding yourself as a writer.

8. Take whatever your daily word count is and devote it *exclusively* to this one story. Do not stray or wander or anything. Do not start multiple stories. Write a 5000-word story to completion.

We are getting close now to you actually embarking on writing a book. But we need to make sure you can actually sustainably write long stories. So, don't just do this exercise once, keep doing it. Keep doing it until 5000 words doesn't seem like nearly enough, and that you find you can't even fit your ideas within that word count limit.

Also, fun fact, at this point, if you've got this far, then you're a real writer.

All who write are writers, but if you can do this step, then you are a full-blown short fiction writer. And that is not at all something to sneeze at or diminish.

You're one of us now, and I'm glad to invite you to our ranks. I'm proud of you.

Really, I am.

Now let's train you into the author you always wanted to be.

A MISTAKE
NEW WRITERS MAKE

One would assume the way one might **tell** a story, or describe an idea, is the same way you would write it.

It's such a mental leap to realize the way you **tell** a story is to **show**, by walking through the world/situation you created, that the new writers **tell** without realizing the error.

And, really, can you blame them? Writing something good takes a shit ton of practice, and world-building is a skill high on the totem pole of difficulty. So, why *wouldn't* they just think you can dump the way the world works on the reader's head? It seems easy. It seems economical.

But it is wrong.

Showing is better, not **telling**.

The oldest bit of advice in the playbook. The sometimes-contested concept.

But if you're going to break rules, you better have a damn good reason. And, even then, make sure you're not just being lazy about your creation.

Because it is easy to just **tell**.

Telling is saying the world is inside a bubble. **Showing** is having a character spend time looking out a window and marveling at the bubble. Seeing it. Being an outsider questioning it, looking at its parts. That's **showing**.

And **showing** is the best way to do most things even for reasons some might not get right away. Like, when I started out, my stories were...well: too short. **Telling** *is* economical—it cuts down on word count. And when you want to write an entire book, **showing** is not only a better choice to make your reader feel the world is real—it's also the best way to hit the touted 50,000-word minimum it takes for a novel.

So, **show**, don't **tell**. And though if you're new at this you may not be able to do it right away, it's a thing worth practicing.

It's a thing that makes a good story.

HOW TO DIALOGUE

"So, what is that? That massive white mass?"

"What? That? Oh, that's the pile of salt I bought to illustrate a point."

"Really, Brandon?"

"Yep—made sense at the time."

"How the heck did you afford such a thing?"

"Eh, you don't want to know. It involves more mustard than you thought reasonable and a howler monkey I like to call Bob."

"You just wrote it into existence, didn't you?"

"Okay, yeah. But it shows what I need them to know. My advice, especially *this* advice, is more so than usual just my opinion: and they need to know that if they are reading this."

"Okay, well, point made. So, what are we talking about this time, Brandon? Are you still hammering away at teaching writing tips?"

"I am. I haven't hit every topic yet, after all. And today I am talking about dialogue, and how to write it—or at least a way to go about it."

"Is that why you have this all as dialogue? Are you being meta again?"

"Yes, yes I am. It's kind of one of my favorite things, and all dialogue seemed like a fun gimmick."

"Emphasis on the word 'gimmick.'"

"Oh, quiet you—but not really. This call and response thing makes the game more fun. So, here's what I can say about dialogue. First off—"

"Wait! Aren't you going to talk about how dialogue is a tool, and not to rely on it too much to set things up for the reader? That you need a combo of it and description to get across a scene?"

"Well, now I have. Thanks, fake conversation partner. So, as I was going to say: in fiction at least, the dialogue has a goal. I call it the 'punch line,' though it need not be funny. Or even come at the end of a joke."

"So, then, why call it that?"

"Well, I don't have an exact reason for using that term. But it feels right. And, here's the point: in real life, chit-chat is sometimes random and useless and exists to pass the time. But a book, a story, is a piece of entertainment: so, don't just dump all this random stuff on their heads, and then expect them to go through the slog."

"So, it has to have a purpose?"

"Yeah, exactly. Right on the money, my illustrative buddy. When you start a line of dialogue, when two characters go at it verbally—no matter the context—know how the conversation ends when you begin writing it. What it reveals, what it builds towards, and what you want to achieve. A conversation can have multiple punch lines and can hit one then work to set up another."

"That's one way to think of it."

"It's *my* way of thinking of it. I lay the groundwork, I set the verbal habits of the players, and I know what it builds toward. Good interplay of dialogue will read— even if containing a ton of deviation and interruptions (and in fact maybe more so when it does)—like a dance and poem coming from many mouths. All going toward the point of the conversation. There's a winner, a loser, a battle, in every talk. Combatants racing for who gets the last word, and who leaves the biggest scar or spot of light on the entire enterprise."

"That sounds hard."

"Not really. Ever wanted to ask someone out on a date, or for a favor? Or anything like that? No matter what the goal, even at the point of opening pleasantries, you are moving toward it, psychically. Yanking the line toward the endpoint. You are setting up a delivery, without alerting the receiver quite yet to the destination."

"That's kind of cool."

"Isn't it, though?"

ON KILLING CHARACTERS

"I put a pair of stainless-steel steak knives from my thirteen-piece cutlery set through their fucking hearts."

-Sales Rush by Brandon Scott

"Something *intimate*. Something I had to dig for, rip into and pry from her. I wanted to see her soul. And I wondered how red that ebony skin was going to get before I found it."

-Waking Nightmares by Brandon Scott

"He stops. Cerebral fluid draining on the rich mahogany wood."

-Piano Player by Brandon Scott

I kill characters. I murder them. Butcher them. I delight in the well set-up destruction of a fictional person I created.

I admit it readily: I am a killer of characters. As serial as they come.

And I am not alone. Among the great destroyers of protagonists and fictional people are the likes of George

R. R. Martin, William Shakespeare, and even—if you think about it—J.K. Rowling.

Death is, and always was, a massive part of fiction. Because there is no more basic, primal fear than death. And damn is it good to create drama.

And while there might be plenty of lists online talking about why you should kill a character, and why you shouldn't sometimes, I am going to talk about something different. I am going to tell you about *how* you kill a character. What you should at least consider when you decide that Joe Protagonist needs a spike through his head.

IT'S THE END

Like THE END. As in, the character does not get to be around anymore. Exactly like you can never see a dead person again, you don't get to write a character once he disappears. No matter how attached you might be to them, once you decide they are gone: THEY. ARE. GONE.

And please don't cheat and bring someone back from the dead. It immediately cheapens the character's efforts. It makes it so all the things they lost or fought for don't matter as much. It makes the danger less, the drama less, when you know that they can undo a loss.

HAPPY ENDINGS AND CHARACTER

DEATHS ARE NOT THAT DIFFERENT.

At least, not in execution. Like I said above, it is the end of the character. Everything they did, every choice they made, led them to this moment. So, treat it as such. Even if it's quick, brutal, or unexpected—give them the honor of letting it be the end of their story. Let them die doing something they cared about or getting in a line of dialogue. Even if the character just dies getting drunk and accidentally falls off a bridge, let them have some humanity. Some semblance of being alive before you cast them aside.

Death is the end of a character arc. However small.

THE BODY NEVER LEFT

I am not here to get into a religious debate—so I'm not even going to touch the concept of what happens to the identity of a person when they die. But I do know, without a doubt, that the corpse is still around. It's still laying there after the head explodes from the accidental zombie-intended shotgun blast. And characters—people—still care about that body. However illogical, they will still treat it like their friend, like the person's still there.

And don't you dare forget that. What you do with the body of your character after you kill him is of vital importance. Does his body fall out of the helicopter after the sniper shot him? Does something eat him?

Burying the dead is a form of closure. It's a way to say goodbye. And people naturally want that or an equivalent. So, they will go back for the body if they can. And it's often a more devastating scene if they can't.

There's a weight, and a smell, and a piece of matter to a dead character. Even after everything. Use it. Understand it. You are responsible for bringing this fake person to life. So have respect—however small— for his death. Even if the story itself doesn't.

"I can't look away from my arm. I can't stop watching the encroaching sickness creep through my cells, rotting them, twisting them. I can't stop looking even when the blood pool rises around me, engulfing my hair, filling up my throat, and turning my vision black."

-*Plague Ground* by Brandon Scott

WRITING WITH MUSIC PLAYING: A PRO AND CON LIST

While writing in private, alone, is often a necessity, doing so in a quiet location is another matter altogether. Sure, I don't think people write well while a television or the crackle of video games is in the background, but I know some enjoy writing with music in their ears.

And my opinion on this matter has changed over time. As when I first began, I tried not to listen to music while I was doing the actual writing—but thinking about the topic beforehand was fair game for tunes. And then, later, I came to rely on it, as my writing location got more and more distracting. I had noise-canceling headphones and a preset playlist.

But, once I could move to a spot where I had a quiet place to write, I tried to do it with the music not in my ears, but around me from speakers. For a little while, I did it without music at all. But, this, due to whatever reason, flowed into listening to music with headphones yet again.

I'm listening as I write this, in fact. Some pop-punk anthem. My favorite type of music. Fast and punchy and full of drums and guitar. When people ask me what kind of music I like to listen to, I usually respond with something like: "Pop music. Pop-punk music. Rock music both old and new. Something with a fast tempo, something that makes it hard to hear my own thoughts."

But that's just me. But if I had to give advice on the topic, here's what I might offer to the person questioning. A pro and con list. Short and to the point.

Pros:

- If the music fits the mood of the thing you are working on, it might make it easier to picture the movement and rhythm of the scene.
- If, like I was, you are in a situation where it's loud around you, the structure of a song—especially one you already know all the lyrics to, or a song that has no lyrics—will make it easier to think. Random noises are way more distracting than predicted ones.
- It makes writing feel like a faster activity. The word count jumps as you get lost in the sensation and the motion—at least from my experience. Almost like a trance.
- In the same vein as the last bullet point, it might make you type quicker. I realize that sounds somewhat silly, but if the music is fast enough and my body is getting into the process of writing, I find I'll speed up to match the rhythm of the song. Which, on occasion, got me to write 1500 words in only 45 minutes (my current record). It might work for you as well.

Cons:

- If you like the currently playing song enough, you might sing along. And though humans, nowadays, can juggle a lot of plates, singing and listening and thinking and writing all at once is not easy, and out of all the plates, you might drop the writing one. This also applies if you begin to dance a bit in your chair—which *can* happen, trust me.

- It's hard to keep your mind on the volume of the song, and it's *too* easy to crank it overly loud for your ears.

- Getting distracted and trying to find the proper song for something or flipping through a playlist *does waste time*. Having an updated and well-curated playlist can help, but it's still going to be an issue.

- It is much easier for a person to sneak up on you if you do this. You are not, I repeat *not*, aware of your surroundings. Just keep that in mind if you are expecting someone. Or a delivery. Or if you are inside a coffee shop or similar.

Well, there, all the data I can think of to give. Use it to help decide what works best for you. But just remember that though rituals can help, never rely on them to get creative. Music can be an inspiration but should not be a crutch.

AN INTROVERT ARTIST'S ATTEMPT AT BEING MORE OPEN WITH HIS AUDIENCE

Here's my problem: I'm scared to be more personal. But, like any relationship, like any friendship, you must be open with people—or you will not get anywhere. And, being open means being open to the possibility of pain. You can't be emotionally hurt by people if you are not exposed enough to be loved.

And, well, blogging is not unlike that. I am, right now, doing what I am comfortable with.

Sharing what of me I feel I can. And sending it out there for people to see.

But, with that said, I'm not super comfortable with this social media world we live in right now. I don't mind sharing in person. I'm an open individual generally—were we to talk face-to-face—but I also know what a danger the internet can be.

So, I don't post as many status updates as I could. Not as many pictures as I could. Most writers—I'm sure—can agree with this mindset. As can any less-social person. Introverts are well, introverted: having little shells that we crawl into some days and from which we do not want to leave for a while. And, unless one is patient, that can be deterring to the people who want to talk to us.

It can make others not want to interact with us at all.

And, while not everyone is lonely when alone, a lot are. Even introverts. Social creatures, us humans exist as— even if some of us are not as much as others.

And, funny enough, from a creative perspective, that whole "write what you know" thing doesn't always work well because of this. It leads the introvertive creative toward creating things about thinking and pondering and being in one's own head. Which, as I'm sure you can imagine, is not always the most effective building blocks for entertaining products. The real idea behind that old chestnut is to gather your pain, and sorrow, and happiness and joy, and use those for your art. To pour your feelings and passions into things, but not necessarily yourself as a character. Instead, using what you've experienced, what's been done to you, and what you've done to others, and then relay that through characters perhaps more active than you are. Characters who are different than you, and yet the same. Characters who might resemble you in different ways, that others will see parts of you inside of, but still exist as their own, flawed, perhaps even broken and damaged people.

And, I get that it's terrifying to use your soul as paint. Any artist I see tackling topics like eating disorders, gender dysphoria, racism, etc.—when they have personal experience with it—I think are the bravest people in the whole goddamn world.

Because I don't think I can do that. Not as I am.

I don't think I could ever be that open—I'm too closed off, too protective of myself. As a horror writer and an enthusiast of darker media, people give me odd looks sometimes when I talk to them about what I'm curious about and passionate about and want to understand on a deeper level.

So—through that, and perhaps because of the way men are told to be in America—I got trained (via social osmosis) to be closed off. To not show strong feelings or emotions, only traits like wit, machismo, or brooding. But, as I recently relearned again when I posted the "When You Walk Every Day" article, the more open I am, the more people respond. Upon reflection, it turns out that most people's lives are similar. We all have similar pains and similar joys.

I mean this in the best way possible, but you, and I, are not the first to experience sadness so deep it physically hurt, pain so hot it seared the mind, and disgust and apprehension and anxiety and fear so static and vibrating it made being alone seemed the only safe place to be—even if that is, of course, usually a lie.

Deep sigh

Yikes, all right, that was heavy. But, I guess, to share, to communicate, to have honest relationships physically or online, we should share heavy stories like that—at least in small parts.

And, for the sake of art, I'll endeavor toward it.

But, understand, it is difficult for me.

THE BATTLE FOR BOOKS

Being a writer in 2017 is not easy. We have competition and not just from our fellow wordsmiths. How can a book compete with streaming sites and movies? I mean, I love books, duh, and I read a lot of them, but even I am a lover of movies. How could you not love movies? They're so good lately.

Every medium of art has its strong suits, though. Books put out much more than a movie in terms of internal thought and themes. The visual medium cannot—easily at least—show abstract thoughts and internal change like a book can. Most major artforms tell stories, but a book is the most detailed way of presenting a tale.

But, I mean, really, the other art forms are not the problem, but it is fucking unfortunate many people don't take in books like they used to. Even I don't read as voraciously as I did when I was a little kid.

Even for me, sometimes it's hard to find the time.

But and I know this is a little predictable of a call to arms, we need to again. Books can be in other forms; they can be audio; they can be on your phone or your tablet. The act of using one's mind to process words and derive complex situations from descriptions and create fictional people in one's imagination is a skill we must not lose.

Because it *is* a skill, not just a triviality. In a movie, you have the characters represented by living or animated people—some of the work is done for you. And, that's pleasant, do not get me wrong. But it is also a worthwhile exercise to get your mind strengthened now and again by the weight of words.

And, yeah, I know I'm preaching to the choir here. I'm sure you can name off the top of your head some if not many benefits reading has, but I think I also wrote this for myself.

Because I am always making more words for others to read, and I love that I get to do that. Even when it is hard, I'm glad I have this ability and I get to wield it. But that doesn't mean I don't worry about the future of the written word.

Especially its financial future. I want people to keep buying books, both for my own benefit and so kids grow up with the joys of reading.

We are living in an artistic golden age, honestly. The Second Renaissance. Like I wanted. But books fulfill a unique need and *can* coexist with the other types of art. It won't be a proper renaissance without books. They *shouldn't* be left behind.

Or, really, I just hope they aren't.

THE SECOND RENAISSANCE

I'm hesitant to bring this up. I'm not sure if I can properly cover this in an article. It's special to me, and precious, and exactly the sort of thing you're supposed to share with people.

It's a belief I have. An idea that a friend of mine gave me the seeds to think with. And it's big, and it involves all of you.

Because if you're watching the developed world's stage, there's an underlying general...push. Taylor Swift, believe it or not, was the first indicator for me. Her push for fair pay when it comes to her songs made me finally sure it was already starting.

And I know I'm being vague here, but I need you to understand at least part of the logic chain before I can get to the point. So, bear with me, okay?

And the next bit is YouTube. There are so many people on it now, creators who make a living off of it. It's expanding, and kind of incredible. And some are now fighting under the phrase "Where's The Fair Use" for YouTube to protect their artistic freedoms.

And then more and more. I know so many people whose dream is to become an artist. And the platforms are there, websites and streaming and all of these places supporting them. Patreon being a definite big one for giving them livable pay and a support platform. And even in the mainstream, the normal stuff, movies, and television—even children's cartoons—are embracing a deeper level of creative activity. People are calling this another Golden Age of Television.

And like a conspiracy theory, it clicks when you look at it. And makes me excited and hopeful. Because I don't think anyone needs to have someone tell them that the world is in bad shape. But in response we're creating more art, trying to fix things through art.

And it leads me to one conclusion. And the knowledge of it is a big thing that keeps me going as an artist.

And I call it the "Second Renaissance." And you're a part of it, and I'm a part of it. And so many beautiful creations and brilliant creators are a part of it. It's only in its infancy, and that's why I'm telling you about it. Because I want you to know, that if I'm right, that if the signs are what I think they are, you are not just creating art, and chasing immortality, you are contributing to saving this planet.

Because a more beautiful world is so much harder to blow away through nuclear bombs and chemical warfare. As cliché and trite as it may sound, art might be our salvation.

So, I need you to go forward, if you believe in me, and make as much art as you can. And chase being able, if you're not already, to do it as your life. Every time someone successful or popular shows themselves to be a positive force for artistic respect—like I hope you are—it spreads it further.

And I think it might lead to a sort of paradise on earth. So please spread the message.

I'm trusting you with this. Thank you for listening.

Assignment 3:

Yes, now, we are actually going to write a book. The thing you bought this book for, the whole reason we embarked on this endeavor, is almost here.

But we have some prep work to do, and a few more references to read, and then we will get into the nitty-gritty of this.

So, here's your third assignment, and it's not such a hard one.

1. Make a spreadsheet or get some lined paper (or make lined paper if you have to do so).
2. Label that spreadsheet the name of the book that this entire time you've been itching to write. Some authors don't give their books names until most of it is written. I don't agree with this: having a name for it, even if you change it later, solidifies the book in your mind as an object that you might one day make real.
3. Take a minute to just think, and breathe, and mentally prepare yourself for what an adventure you are about to undertake.
4. If you are the type that needs to be held accountable, then find someone you absolutely trust and tell them that you are committing to writing this book, and, if they are willing, tell them to check in on you occasionally to make

sure you're doing it. Don't post it to social media, don't blog about it. It's too early and too fragile for such attention.

5. Do not tell *anyone* the details of your plot. Talking is telling a story, and the story you are going to tell should be on the page, not in the air.

6. Read the next article, it will tell you what to do next. Don't read past the next article until you have done this assignment.

7. Once you have done this assignment, once you've got a roadmap, read on to the next few articles. They'll be things about the creative process, and how to keep motivated as you go through. I want you to have the right mental state before you even begin, and the discipline ingrained long before you need it to survive.

HOW TO OUTLINE
OUTRAGEOUSLY FAST

This is my opinion. This is not a provable science. This is how I do it now, and I find it effective.

If you don't like artistic things being too mechanical, this will not work for you.

But, that said, do you want to outline and organize a new novel fast?

Then read on.

Have an Idea!

I don't know why you're reading this if you don't already know what the book is about. Figure that out first!

Work Out Your Desired Word Count!

Oh, yeah, most people don't tell you to do this. But like I said, this method is a *tad* mechanical. A short novel is 50,000-60,000 words. A normal novel is around 70,000-80,000. Anything higher than that is a little risky when it comes to a publisher. If you're self-publishing: do whatever amount you want. But work out what that amount is!

Figure Out Your Minimum Chapter Size!

This one might take experimentation. You need an accurate gauge of how many words you feel you can use in a chapter without sounding long-winded. I'm a firm believer that a chapter is the equivalent of one movie scene. If you switch locations or the perspective moves, it's a new chapter. So, figure out how many words those are for you.

Math!

I know writers typically aren't fans of math. Or at least *I'm* not. But you should have access to a calculator, so work this out.

How many chapters do you need? If you feel you can only write 500 words for each given portion, then at 50,000 words you're looking at 100 chapters. Which is fine. But you need to know the number.

As a side note, this is not as precise as I'm making it sound. You can shrink and expand and change at any point. The purpose is to make a helpful blueprint for a book so you can focus more on the actual building.

More Numbers!

Work out, right now, how many perspective characters you will have. These are the characters that the narrator will follow. If you're doing first person and switching who's talking each chapter, this is especially important.

If your villain gets his/her/its/their own chapter, this is *also* important. Any flashbacks, any perspective jumps, any prologs, epilogs, artistic whatever's. Figure that shit out early.

Spreadsheet!

Break out a spreadsheet, or a lined piece of paper. Here is where your book meets the light of day.

Here's where you get to be creative.

Put a line for each chapter. If there's more than one perspective, then label which perspective in the first column of the line. If the date or time or location is important, that goes in the next column of the line.

Now, describe in a *single* sentence what happens in each chapter and write it down in the correct line. Keep in mind how many chapters you have to fill, and how many words you feel you can get into one chapter.

If you have to rework or come up with new things for your outline, that's fine.

If you have to remove stuff because it doesn't fit with everything, that's also fine.

And don't worry, you can revise this anytime, and I think you will end up diverging from the original plan at least once.

This is all okay.

And by the end of it, it should look like the plot of a novel. It should feel like it's yours. It should be an exhilarating feeling.

Bonus: Writing Tips!

You already have your outline. So, this part is just a bit of advice. I recommend writing one of your chapters a day. That way momentum picks up, and you don't lose the spark of what you intended.

And if you find yourself lost at any point, you always have that outline to look back at for help.

It's a roadmap from your past self.

That is the beauty of an outline.

SMILE, NOD,
AND KEEP ON WRITING

When the doubts set in, and other artistic pursuits seem easier.

Smile, Nod, and Keep on Writing.

When you feel the sting of every imperfect sentence and line in a story.

Smile, Nod, and Keep on Writing.

When you're tired. When you can't muster the will. When a voice in your head says you can take off one night.

Smile, Nod, and Keep on Writing.

When someone insults your writing and tries to rip away a piece of you.

Smile, Nod, and Keep on Writing.

When you hear of someone else's failure and think "he couldn't, how can I?"

Smile, Nod, and Keep on Writing.

When you read a book and compare it to your work. And yours falls short.

Smile, Nod, and Keep on Writing.

When the world offers such plentiful distractions. A shiny new story, or a different project to do.

Smile, Nod, and Keep on Writing.

When the world shows how cruel it can be to new artists. When the world shows how little it understands us. When non-artists decide they know more about the craft than you. When an internet critic's only goal is to make you feel terrible. When the voices of naysayers grow to a fever pitch.

Say it with me:

Smile, Nod, and Keep on Writing.

Because only you can do it. And it's hard, and it takes discipline. But you are a storyteller.

And we live in a world of stories.

IT DOESN'T HAPPEN
ALL AT ONCE

Never good enough is our achievements, are they? Always someone else has done more than us. Made more money, written more. Better computers. Knows more about this or that. Has more disposable income?

Systemic reasons. Personal reasons. Time and effort going towards only so much stuff. Maybe some of it was excuses? Certainly, too much time on social media.

Hey, I get hating that you haven't done what you wanted so far. I get the existential moment of dripping time—of shuffling off a mortal coil. Being so very disappointed in yourself for not being that version of yourself that you see in those passing daydreams. The famous, somehow multi-tasking on another plane of time, shining version of yourself.

I wish I could say that it goes away. That imposter syndrome is not a real, noticeable thing. That modern capitalism won't continue to make you feel like you're never rich enough. That money somehow defines your self-worth and sense of success.

I can tell you one thing though.

You've likely improved.

The tragedy of youth is that we often learn things much later than they would have been useful. Looking back, we see mistakes. Looking back, aren't we so very embarrassed?

A fucking good sign that.

That means you recognize points of error. That you get that you made mistakes. That you *learned*. Oh, cliché and sounds like I'm talking to a child, right? Was it any less true then? If anything, it's truer *now*.

You never stopped skinning your knees. You just stopped doing it on a playground. It may not have "built character," but, hey, you're alive enough. And, really, when did you last skin your knee?

I am not naïve enough to claim anyone can do anything. But I'm not cynical enough to say it's hopeless.

Improvement, especially big life stuff, doesn't happen all at once. You cannot "become an adult" in a week. I don't care if you bought a house, made your own doctor's appointment, and signed up for life insurance all in the same day—it's not going to undo that uncertainty.

It's a slow thing.

It's growing. Like you did when you were 5. Just because you're not a kid anymore, doesn't mean there's not more to learn.

I can't promise there's satisfaction at the end—I haven't been there to see it. But, at least, at freaking least, in the middle parts, there are moments where you simply *are* luckier than you expected. And you'll be happier again and again than you thought you could be. You'll find there are new thresholds to joy.

Yeah, others got more stuff. More of this or that.

But if we are better than ourselves, a year back, we are going forward. We have matured. Taken those scrapes and hardened up a little against the world.

Do something small towards a goal, each day, each week. Chill out—it'll all be okay.

THIS IS OUR JOB

I'm probably right to assume that a good chunk of the people who read my posts are artists, yeah? I think that's a fair assumption of things.

I hope so, anyway, because I'm addressing you right now. I'm talking to the painters, the writers, the poets, the singers, the animators, and everyone else who makes things for the sake of aesthetics.

Give me your attention for a second.

Because we've got a job to do. This time in history is what we are here for—and we need to step up to the plate.

The doctors, the nurses, the manufacturers, the scientists, they are vastly more important than us presently, but we still have our own job to do.

We need to make art.

But not just any art.

This is when people need our best creations, our most heartfelt stories, our most joyous songs.

I think you can feel the mood of the world becoming dour. People aren't just bored and trapped inside, they are scared, concerned, and tense. It's not healthy, and it's not good for anyone to feel that way.

It ripples, and it spreads, and it does change how society functions.

Thus, our task: to put forward creations and art that inspires, that amazes, that makes people laugh. I'm primarily a horror writer, and I have a dark sense of humor, but when I can, where I can, I'm trying to tell tales that make the world not seem so bleak.

There's likely still a long road ahead for this virus, and, though perhaps we can't be the ones healing those sick, we can keep hope alive. Even if all we can serve as is a distraction, we're still doing our job.

And it *is* our job, and we cannot ignore it.

If you're an artist, be an artist. The world needs you.

I need you.

SOME MORE MOTIVATION

Sometimes these posts are just as much for me in the future as they are for you guys.

This is one of those.

Because I know I will meet moments where I need a little pep talk, and thus I will store that pep talk in the one place I know I'll find it.

And if it helps other artists out there, well, all the better.

All right. So, if you're reading this, that means you are currently tired. A little sore. I imagine the carpal tunnel settled in, or it's around 2 AM and you haven't made your word count yet.

Or all of those things at once.

Well, first off dude, it would not be the first time. Hell, do you remember that night someone found you walking back and forth typing poetry into your phone at way-too-late-o'clock? Just because you didn't make your word count with the story you were working on that day?

Yeah, and do you remember how that went the last time? You were fine. You did it. You caught up on your sleep, eventually. And you kept that writing streak in for another day.

So you can do it. I know you can. The words don't stop. As long as you live a life with interesting things happening, you will not run out of words.

So, chill out.

You can always edit later. So just go. Pound your fingers at those keys.

People might hate it?

Ha. So what?

It's junk?

You can always edit it later.

I'm so tired.

You can *always* edit it later.

Just keep going. Smile, nod, and keep on writing.

Do it to hold up the Second Renaissance.

Do it because you need to write every damn day!

Do it for all the artists you poured your soul into making sure they didn't feel like they were alone.

Do it for your fans, however small in number.

Do it for yourself.

Stop arguing.

And god damn chase a dream, Brandon.

Because I am proud of you.

I am *so* proud of you.

You're stronger now than you thought you ever could be.

You're a writer. So, let's do what we're here to do on this planet.

Assignment 4:

For real this time.

The book.

You are ready to write a book.

If you have followed all my instructions, internalized all the words I've said about discipline and it being something important and powerful and how much good writing is just hard work, then you are one of the lucky few out of the many who make the attempt that can, and probably will, write a book and publish a book.

So, my fellow author, it's time to get to work.

By now you already know what you must do, but I'll spell it out for you.

1. Write your word count every day.
2. Don't give up, don't take a day off (unless someone dies or something equally dramatic).
3. Make redundant and even further redundant backups of everything you write. Don't let computer failure stop you from this goal. Back it up daily and keep your backups safe.
4. Try not to second-guess yourself too much.
5. Don't stop even if you're bored.

6. And keep writing, writing, writing, until the book, the whole damn book, from start to finish, is done.

7. Have a little celebration. You earned it. Your job is not done, but you've earned some party and some joy and some acknowledgment of being a real author who does work and doesn't just talk about it.

The following articles are for you as you do this. They are loosely related topics that will address various things you might experience as you go through the process of authorship. They can be read casually, as needed, and whenever you have the time. The most important thing right now is that you get the word count done and that you keep up the routine.

The routine is *everything*.

The articles are just here for when you need them.

The next assignment is for when you get to the other end. It is for your finished manuscript.

I'm looking forward to sharing that with you.

"I'VE LOST CONTROL OF MY CHARACTERS!"

"Bobby, tell the doctor what you said to me."

"…I had…have voices in my head. They talk to each other."

"Is that all?"

"No… no. I can't help but listen to people secretly, and I try to remember how they said things. I see random parts of things I don't really understand. Actions, faces…that sort of stuff. Like a scene from a movie. I don't always know what they mean."

"Okay…tell me, Bobby, do you read?"

"Yes…a lot."

"Is that bad, doctor? I could take away his books."

"No, not bad…just a sign. And taking away the books would only make it worse—not that it is bad, okay? Bobby, one other question for you, and you don't have to worry about if your answer is wrong or not, I just want to help you: when you daydream, what do you see?"

"…I see worlds. I see things move and talk. I see outcomes to things that are not there—I know they are fake, but they are better than what's real. Or, sometimes, much worse."

"Is he sick, do you think?"

"No, I've seen this before. He's a writer. It's terminal—but not an illness. I suggest you get him some paper fast. If he hasn't started yet, he will. And it will consume him."

And, that, my friends, is how you do a preposterously long lead-in to talking about the idea that stories flow out of a creator, and, in a way, we lose control of them. That's what has been happening to me lately: I don't have control of my stories anymore. I outline, and I set boundaries, and I plan an ending, but beyond that, the characters don't listen much. They willfully go against my plans, and at the end of it: I get their logic. They often move toward the ending I planned more gracefully than *I* could ever choreograph.

My stories are not fully mine anymore. I just kind of "represent" *for* them.

Heck, characters sometimes even *die* when I still needed them. They just…died. I could not save them.

And without the certainty of control over things, all I understand is my patterns. My tropes. The rules the unfurling tapestry happens to follow. Totally determined by me—but beyond of what I am conscious.

And if this is happening to you, then the advice I can offer is to roll with it. We can't do anything to stop the lightning and the thunder and the hurricanes and the laws of entropy and gravity. All we can do is try to understand why, and how, and prepare ourselves. And then clean up the mess left over and make what we can of the debris.

Your and my dreams are spilling out, and that is okay: write as your fingers do it for you. The world needs dreamers. And when things are hard, cripplingly hard even, the world of imagination is one to which everyone should have access. So, share your bursting self-determined imagination. Because your creations may save someone from storms, from villains, or even from their own darkness—not controlled either.

DON'T WORRY SO MUCH

I'm a worrywart. Not anxious so much as just very aware of my surroundings—and I've seen too many people spill their drinks. A long time ago, I developed this habit of sneakily handling things. I'll subtly move objects away from the edge, adjust plugs so that they can't short out, and quietly circumvent stuff that might cause people to get mad at each other.

As many times ranted, I know my way around chaos, and I know how it seems to work, so, if not me, then who else is going to do subtle acts to keep that chaos from hurting people, from ruining days?

But that doesn't mean I don't mess up in other ways.

I'm not great at conversations sometimes. I'm not great at "normal human" stuff. I can set up an automated system across my entire room so that it remains the optimal temperature and light—but I'm no good at small talk.

Hell, I'm a horror writer. Sometimes it's hard to recall that to some people talking about the monster from a horror movie and the symbolism behind how it works and how it kills victims is an upsetting topic.

I can be too callous, too crass, too ranting, or simply not considerate of someone's potential worldview. I'm a diehard politically correct person—and I maybe judge people too harshly who aren't also.

I'm a professional movie critic. I have strong opinions—but I sometimes present them in a way that upsets, and I hate when I accidentally tear down a piece of media special to someone.

But what is the point of all this complaining and self-belittling you may rightfully be asking?

Well, it's because, with all of this, I probably worry too much. I probably check unnecessarily to make sure I'm not yet again doing something that might upset. I don't do this all the time—but more than needed.

I'm used to living in my head. It's where all my work is done before my fingers even hit the keyboard, before a plan comes to fruition—but I'm so used now, I think, to looking for little problems, little errors, in grammar, in routines, in automation, that it's hard to turn off and I really *should* sometimes turn it off for a little while.

Because things do work out, oddly. They do more often than I ever expected. People are *way* more forgiving than I think school teaches us to expect. So long as you are kind and genuine, people often will forgive mistakes.

There actually are very few truly hopeless situations, so long as you have ideas for solutions and a willing grit to go for them.

So, I need to worry less. Not overthink it sometimes. There's sometimes just too much in the world in need of enjoying to wonder if you accidentally pissed someone off earlier that day.

JUST SO YOU KNOW, NOBODY REALLY KNOWS WHAT THEY ARE DOING

I don't really know the age group that reads my posts. But, in case you are a young person like me—and you feel stressed out and worried and anxious about your future—I have something to tell you.

People have no idea what they are doing.

Your parents. Your teachers. People on the street. They only know what they bothered to learn. People are talented and knowledgeable, sure—but on only certain things.

Something no one has worked out perfectly is how to be a human on earth.

You can't specialize in that—there are too many pieces.

We are all winging it.

I realize that to some, if you have not heard that idea before, it might be a bit daunting. A stressful act to look around and find the world is propped up by billions of people who are faking it until they make it.

But, two points to that.

One: the world has yet to end.

And two: that means that humans are much better than anyone ever thought.

Think about it.

Science and spaceships and cookie dough ice cream and mural paintings and interpretive dance and storytelling and computers and music were all made by *people*. We got to this point in history by letting people bumble around until they found something, they were good enough at that it was worth letting them continue.

That's bonkers.

We basically "accidented" progress.

We made up money.

We created every language.

Every recipe for every food was invented by people.

Your *name* is a random assortment of sounds that we decided sounded good. I am speaking to you through what was basically millions of human's efforts combined. The endeavors of discovery, dedication, and then accidentally amazing results.

We are all winging it, all teetering on the edge of abject failure, and we all still manage to do what we do and make every business and building and light you see around you somehow run and work within the confines of entropy and cosmic indifference.

If we can do that, then you can survive.

You can be happy.

I have no idea how anyone is happy, but we manage somehow.

Love and songs exist despite how fucking tiny we are—and how short life is.

Perhaps we are all laughing in the dark.

But at least we are not alone.

WHAT DO I DO IF I FEEL LONELY AND SAD AND TRAPPED INSIDE WHILE WRITING?

Explore the world. That's the big thing people want to do. And, it's the same with me. But, there's something to be said about the pleasures of knowing one's home well, of being in a single location for a long enough time to understand the place, not just travel through it.

And that's what I want to talk about here.

I walk, a lot. In the same general area. And, when you do such a thing, something you might not expect happens.

People you do not know notice you walking and remember you.

People wave at me. Smile and nod and give happy-to-see-me greetings. I don't know their names. They have no real idea who I am. But they've seen my face enough times now that they recognize me.

I like to imagine they even miss me when I am walking somewhere else. I miss *them*, that's for sure. When a house goes on the market in my neighborhood, I wonder where they have gone.

While growing up, it's a connection I never thought I'd have. When I'm lonely, when I'm walking with just myself and some music for company, it's nice to recall that linking of humanity, and how I fit into it.

Life is so much bigger than us. So many people…it's outrageous. All going their own ways. Only glimpsed at in passing. The news makes the world so scary; you know? But a walk, even the same walk in the same place a thousand times, reminds me it's not all bad out there.

There's still beauty. Nature is not all gone. Clean air, and storm clouds, and blue sky. Life is still with us on Earth. And, people, people really are good and worth the effort.

So, I'll see you on the sidewalks. And I'll be sure to wave.

"THIS WRITING IS SO DEPRESSING!"

If you are reading this, and consider yourself a supremely serious person, then I have a thing to say to you.

Lighten up!

Honestly, just smile.

Here, I'll help: look around and make sure you are in a good place to do this (free of prying ears or eyes) and smile super wide. I don't care if it is the fakest smile you have ever smiled. Do it even if the act makes your skin stretch—unless that would be legitimately harmful to your face, then don't.

Now, hold that expression, and bark out a laugh. Echo that fucker.

Good, you look like a psycho. But I bet you cheered yourself up a bit. Or, at least, the mental picture I conjured in your head for this shenanigan did.

It is, after all, a silly thing to do. To imagine doing.

But whoever said being silly was bad?

Because it's not.

Let me say something, a digression: I write dark things. Not new news if you read my flash fictions.

In fact, I create dark enough stuff that people challenge me to write full-on happy stories. My response: "sounds boring." But, even still, with all my macabre fixation, that does not mean I won't occasionally write romance stories. Or bittersweet human drama stuff. It also means I can and will try to interject some humor into what I do.

When you talk about writing bleak worlds and people, when you say a summary of the plot of a dark story, it does not always come across that though the subject might be heavy the delivery doesn't have to be.

Let me put this in another way: the end of the world, when you really think it over long enough, is *kind* of funny. Or it can be. I listen to enough comedy routines to know the entire spectrum of human misery and strife can be presented in a way light and airy and flippant.

And sure, if done wrong, even a little wrong, you stand to offend people who have had their lives destroyed by these terrible things. People who have every right to not find morbid jokes funny. But, for the rest of us, there's use in funniness among the darkness and seriousness.

It's a curious thing. I could show you stories about what might happen if a nuclear bomb was ever allowed to go off on this planet again. Burning bodies—I could describe it to you in detail.

And for a little while that will horrify. But assuming you don't go insane, you will become desensitized to it. Because the concept of nuclear annihilation is not something you should hold in your head for too long.

And apathy is not a recipe for preventative action.

But if I make the same sort of story just a *bit* funny… if I make you laugh and then the implications sink in, I think it will change something in you, in a healthier way.

So, lighten up, if only to make your point sink in more. And, also, because being grim all the time isn't good for your health.

There's a reason a person is bright and flush with life, while a corpse is gray and pale and dull.

HOW TO MAKE A MONSTER

#1: Pick a Fear

Ideally, monsters are scary. And while big claws and sharp teeth do cause some emotional response, it's shallow, and often not enough. Instead, to build a proper monster, you need to start with a fear. A specific fear. It can be anything really, but the more personal it is to you, the more you can bring it out.

Here are some basic suggestions to get you started:

- Loneliness
- Disease
- Torture
- Darkness
- Death
- Insects

Chosen one? Something deep, dark, and personal? Are your insides squirming with the thought of it? Are you desperately trying to think of anything else but the implications of that fear? Good. Now it's time to give it action.

#2: Make it Hunt

Did you know vampires, among other things, represent sexually transmitted diseases?

So, how do they hunt? Vampires charm you. In most stories, they are suave, seductive creatures, and lure you to a bite. And then you're either changed forever or just flat dead. A bit extreme, but the point stands: the way your monster kills, hunts, or tortures should reflect the fear they represent.

Zombies isolate you into a house, trapping you in claustrophobia. Werewolves hunt you, like an animal. The boogeyman gets you when you're asleep.

Your monster is a physical embodiment of a fear. So, it should also cause that same fear in a person. By whatever sadistic means necessary.

#3: Give it Skin

This step might not even be necessary. If you did the last two to the best of your abilities, the creature might just jump into your head fully formed.

But for those who don't now have a monster stalking through their brainpan, here's a final tip to create your creature.

And that is, you need to decide how real you want it to look. It's a sliding scale. On one end you have your zombies and vampires. They look almost human, but not quite. And the horror comes from the subtle off-ness of the whole thing.

Then if you progress even further, you get the beasts. Often based on some animal (or animals) these usually rely on the sheer frightening nature of something unreasonable. Whatever part of the human mind that remembers being prey latches on to images like that.

And finally, if you want to be a bit out there, you can go with exotic shapes. Sometimes this is simple, like a monster made of smoke or slime. And sometimes it's absolutely insane. A twisted form of anything, and everything you want to throw into it. Fangs, tentacles, thirty eyes, whatever.

A good monster is timeless. So, respect it enough to give it a unique and personal look that resonates with you. Because then it will resonate with your audience.

"I'M WRITING HORROR AND I CAN'T GET IT SCARY ENOUGH!"

I told you, long ago, how to make monsters.

But, now, specifically, I am going to spend a few moments on how to make anything scary.

Everyone is afraid of something.

And, to elicit fear, you only need to hit them in the right spot.

Fear is about loss, ultimately. If you didn't feel like the thing you might lose is worthwhile, there would not be fear attached. Because stories are usually fiction, the most common thing horror tries is losing a likable character.

Sometimes they also "proxy" a real-world death.

Loss of a family member, loss of a friend, loss of a pet, loss of something comforting like home.

And it goes further.

A lot of the most iconic and scary monsters make someone lose even more than their—or someone else's—life. They lose their autonomy. They become another of the monsters. Werewolves, vampires, zombies, ghosts. They all convert. They steal faces, names, identities.

It's all about loss.

So, let's bring it back.

How do you make something scary?

Well, for a human monster, make it take things. Or not have things itself. Humans have a specific way we expect things to look and to be scary you need to make them lose a sense of familiarity, which is ultimately a loss of comfort or safety.

Remove a facial feature or two.

It doesn't have to be physical. Remove empathy. Remove remorse. Remove mercy.

Alternatively, to create a sense of loss of capability or certainty, take away a character's ability to perceive in some way. Or affect things in some way.

Leave them in pitch black. Or deep underground. Or locked in a house.

Show them things out of their control.

A car that won't stop.

A disease with no cure.

A rickety bridge with no safety rails.

You may have heard of cosmic horror. It's the horror that one does not matter. But, really, all horror makes someone feel small, afraid, unimportant. Scurrying away from things that do not consider you worthy of life.

To vampires, we're food. To giants, we are insect-sized annoyances. To dark gods, we might—maybe—be so lucky to be playthings worthy of not breaking.

Humans become calm and certain when we feel we're safe.

So, if you're making horror, continue to shatter that illusion in every way you can.

And, soon enough, someone will start screaming.

I ALREADY HAVE SO MUCH TO DO! HOW AM I GOING TO WRITE THIS?!

Look, I like being able to just chill, too, but, trust me when I tell you this, and it may go against a lot of the thinking people seem to have: but being busy, having a lot to do...is a *good thing*.

I recently, like within the last week or two, tried to double my projects; I drastically increased the number of items on my daily checklist, and, against all the usual "logic" on the matter, want to know what happened?

I got more done. Like, I got the stuff I was doing done, plus the new stuff. Nothing particularly changed in my efficiency, at least in a way that I noticed, but, lo and behold, I am mostly on top of my shit, at least for now.

Sometimes, every so often, I write an article for the purpose of myself reading it later. This blog functions a little like a public journal, diary, or personal guide for me, that maybe helps other people. So, this is advice for me and everyone else who cares to read this: do more. Be more.

If you feel like you're overwhelmed—instead of cutting things out of your life—try to get yourself a few more activities in need of doing. It's better to forget a few of many tasks, then be unwilling to deal with life's needs.

Trust me on this: you can do more than you do, and you can do it without losing what you already do.

We all have so many projects and plans; I'd prefer to get them done.

Assignment 5 and Beyond

I'm sorry to say our time together, in this book, is almost done. I've done what I can. I've given you what I know. It's not easy, it's not glamorous, and it's not for the faint of heart.

If you've done what I've told you—if you put in the hours and hours of work—then you are staring at the first draft of a manuscript.

You may feel protective of this thing you've made. You may feel as though the time to the end of your author's journey is almost upon you. You may be whistling a jaunty tune at your breakout hit of a novel, sure to dazzle.

But this book would not be this book if I did not give you a little more tough love, and honest truths, and frank words.

What I am about to say may sound resoundingly cruel. But it is a tough truth that an author must face.

I faced it, and you must do so as well.

The book you have written is probably not very good yet. First drafts, especially the very first time an author produces their very first draft, is not usually a masterpiece.

Further, it's likely not that great.

It is not even a smidgen close to its completion.

Editing is writing, and what you have created is the raw clay, the core, of a story. Writing this draft was barely a step of it.

For almost no story comes out clean. The ability to get it close on one pass is a skill earned through many, many books written.

You have to edit this book now. By yourself, and then with help. It may take an infinity longer than the writing did, and it may be all the harder.

But, before you despair, I want you to realize that you just *wrote a book*. You achieved a goal a lot of people have and never manage to do.

And the breaking of that seal, that newfound certainty that you can write a book, will give you the power to write many more and to write them fast.

If nothing else, I've given you that power.

Now it's time for the final assignment I have. Because this book is not meant to teach you how to edit a book to completion. There are other better books for that lesson. I may one day write a book on the subject, but for now, here's what I have as advice. Here's my final assignment.

1. Put your book away. Hide it somewhere you will not see it. Forget about your book for a week at least. Go write something new. Don't lose the habits you worked so hard for—but let this book sit and "cool."

2. When you feel as though you can handle it, make a new copy of your manuscript. Physical or digital, it doesn't matter. Just create a second copy of it. This is so you have an original if you make a change you don't like.

3. Start reading it from the beginning. This can count toward the 20 pages a day habit I taught you at the beginning if you want.

4. Fix every error you see, as you see them. I recommend actually reading out loud (or getting software to do it for you) the entire book. If something sounds wrong, then keep reiterating that line until it sounds and *feels* right when you hear it. Then keep going. It may be tedious— but it is necessary work.

5. It is perfectly okay if you end up needing to rewrite aspects of the story from scratch. It is not undoing your work, and you did not waste time. Rewriting is a natural aspect of the process and is not shameful.

6. Every time you go through the entire book and make substantial changes to the story or too

large sections of wording, or any major plot or world details, make sure you finish that readthrough—then start over and read the whole thing through again.

7. At a certain point, and its different for each author, you will need to get this book to someone or preferably a few people that you trust to read over and comment on any plot or character aspects that they think is problematic or wrong or shouldn't be as it is.

8. Do not change things exactly the way these people tell you to change things. If your reader dislikes something, then you did something wrong—but that does not mean they can be trusted to know how to fix the problem. As the author, you must decide what the real issues are that caused that reaction. Do not reject or disregard their criticism, just don't internalize them as inarguable truth.

9. Reiterate (with and without feedback) until you feel that the changes you make are not improvements, just changes. If you feel like you can't stand to read your damn story anymore, that's usually a sign that you're just being a perfectionist and should move on to grammar edits.

10. Only edit for grammar and spelling at the end. If you do it earlier, you might end up changing things and undoing your work. You can hire someone to do this for you.

11. Have on hand at all times a log of how every character's name and unique item name and location name is spelled. Checking to make sure its uniform can and should be its own check.

12. Get an editor. Among some this is a controversial point, but regardless of what some might claim, *for new authors who have never published before you absolutely need a professional editor trained to work in your genre of choice.* And yes, this part can be expensive, but cheap editing is not usually worth the time or the effort. If it is under one hundred dollars ($100) and it is not just proofreading, it's likely not good editing.

13. Make the choice if you are going to pursue an agent or self-publish. Yes, you need to get it pro-edited before either choice. Agents reject unedited manuscripts—so don't think you'll just get someone else to front that bill.

14. Be patient, be brave, and be an author, and go towards publishing. Find books on the subject that are by trusted people and be ready for an adventure.

And that's what I know and what I've learned. This book is a pathway I've made for those ready to walk it and to become serious about being an author of a real book. I hope I did not come off as cruel or callous.

I want more people to become authors and writers. The world, more every day, needs stories and art and language and communication. The task is not one to be taken lightly, or as a passing thought of glory.

For those that will toil in the fiction mines, it is all we can be, and a pleasure to be, and a joy like nothing else.

Thank you for reading this book. I hope for some it is what they needed it to be.

I'll leave you with one last article, one that is important to me. One that changed my life with the writing of it. I hope it might also be useful to you.

To Those Unseen

To those that see a painting in twilight skies.

To those who pour out their heart because they need someone to understand.

To those that push themselves harder—harder—harder, until they find a new way.

To those that don't sleep, don't eat, sacrifice their bodies for the sake of something grand.

To those that explain, again and again, rather than fight.

To those that choose others above themselves.

To those that love.

To those that managed to love themselves.

To those that haven't and yet love others all the same.

To those that wake up with a purpose.

To those that have yet to find it.

To those that strive to teach.

To nurture.

To help.

To make people see the truth.

To save people, without reason.

To those who have a reason.

To those who pray, practice, feel faith.

And want something good for the soul of man.

To those that hold down every evil and destructive impulse and be kind.

I see you.

And I want you to know that while not everyone is what this world calls special.

We have the capacity to be better than that.

We have the capacity to love.

To learn.

To protect.

To save.

To continuously, every day, choose to do the one thing that our hearts know to be right.

I see that you really are trying.

And that you are good—despite how you might feel.

"Special," no.

Extraordinary.

Kind.

Good.

A worthy person.

Better, I think, than being envied.

The best is being loved.

I see you help the world every single time you work to make someone smile.

Your dreams.

Your projects.

Those things that you allow to wander your mind.

I want you to know that there's still time to begin.

You may start on them now.

You may start on them tomorrow.

Even an unfinished song is still a moment of joy in its creation.

And I want to tell you that joy given out always comes back bigger.

It's cyclical.

But I think you knew that already.

ABOUT THE AUTHOR

From a young age, Brandon Scott realized he was tired of stories where all the characters survived, and the good guys always won. And, after flirting off and on with the idea of writing for a few years, he got his first disturbed shudder out of a reader. Since then, Brandon Scott has been chasing that same shudder, penning dark speculative fiction stories of various lengths—some of which even he can't think about for too long without his stomach tightening.

When Brandon Scott is not writing, sleeping, cooking, or just busy with life stuff (a rare thing indeed) he enjoys anime, books, movies, television, dumb online videos, and really anything you might call "nerdy" or "geeky." He lives in Florida and somehow still manages to feel cold.

Manufactured by Amazon.ca
Bolton, ON

21197892R00072